# ALSO CHECK OUT FROM SS REED···

Lab Cat:

A Story Fiction Original


Eight Clouds Express

and Other Story Fiction Originals


SS Reed's Story Fiction:

Volume 1

Volume 2

Volume 3

Volume 4

Volume 5

Volume 6

Volume 7

Volume 8

# TABLE OF CONTENTS

# THE DETECTIVE'S JOURNEY

## A FREE VERSE ESSAY ON CREATIVE INSPIRATION AND ORIGINALITY

To whoever felt drawn to open this book.

*The Detective's Journey*

*A Free Verse Essay on Creative Inspiration and Originality*

Copyright © 2023, 2024 by S.S. Reed.

All rights reserved.



For serious business inquiries, email me at ssreedofficial@gmail.com.

# WHAT IS STORY FICTION?



Time

Space

Reality

Physics

Logic

Human behavior

In the world of Story Fiction,

what you know may not always apply.

Story Fiction, as a genre,

can't be given a formal or official meaning.

Though its voice is meant for everyone to hear

(no matter what age, gender or background),

its words that day may be gifted to you alone.

So then, how would you describe it to others?

Well...

Get cozy in your favorite chair.

Pour yourself a glass of your favorite drink.

Snuggle up in that comfy blanket.


Spend a moment of your time with us.

Explore the world we have to offer.


And ask yourself,

as you walk through this story,

connect with these characters...


...what is the voice speaking to you?

# INDIGO
# SPEAKEASY

## AN INTRODUCTION & WELCOME

# WITH A KEEN EYE FOR DETAILS···

w/ SS REED


...Oh, hi there!

Welcome to the Indigo Speakeasy!


I'm SS Reed.

I run the place.


Come, sit down at the bar,

order yourself a drink, get comfortable.

We can have a chat—if you're open to it.


...There you go.


So, anyways!


You like stories? (I imagine you do if you're here.)

Because I consider myself a bit of a storyteller.


Maybe you've seen some of my work.


*SS Reed's Story Fiction Magazine*

*Lab Cat: A Story Fiction Original*

*Eight Clouds Express and Other Story Fiction Originals*

(...Yeah, there's a reason I explain what Story Fiction

at the beginning of this and each book.)


If you've read one or two (or all) of them,

you may have thought to yourself...


*Wow, this guy sure loves great detectives.*

*And phantom thieves.*


And...no, you wouldn't be wrong.


Along with mad scientists and superheroes,

they're my favorite character archetypes.


I've been inspired by literary characters

like Sherlock Holmes and Arsène Lupin,

manga characters like Conan Edogawa and Lupin III,

and gaming characters like Phoenix Wright and Professor Layton

since I was a kid and teenager.


Over the years, as I grew as a storyteller,

I was inspired by them and did what I could to emulate them, hopefully to create something great that I could call my own.


Funny enough,

when looking at the history of these characters,

I found that many of them often inspire each other.


Like, C. Auguste Dupin inspired Sherlock Holmes,

who in turn inspired

Hercule Poirot, Arsène Lupin and Kogoro Akechi.

And it goes on from there.


...Actually, let's test that.


Almost every creative wants to be original,

they want to be new and unique,

but even the most original ideas

can be compared to some older idea.


What's the key?


Well, let's picture it as a magnificent tree,

a large trunk with plenty of branches, twigs and leaves.

We'll call it...the Great Detective Tree.

What kind of tree is it? Who knows?
Could be a maple tree, a mighty oak
or even a cherry blossom.

The idea of this experiment is to analyze this tree,
starting at the roots,
climbing up the base of the trunk,
tracing out the branches and twigs
and looking at the leaves and fruits.

I first ran and published this experiment
back in June 6, 2023.
Since then, many of these stories have continued to sell,
and several of them even saw a few updates.
I made this new version partially to showcase that.

So, what's a Great Detective?

This is a character so brilliant at solving mysteries
that they can break through cases
that leave the local authorities completely stumped.

Now, this character can work in law enforcement,
but more often than not,

they're either an amateur or work as a private consultant.

In fact, it's often because of their unassuming appearance

that they can get close to the culprit in the first place.


So, a few guidelines to keep us on track:


Not including my starting point,

whatever work follows in the timeline

must cite a previous work

that we saw on the tree as inspiration.

If *Detective Story 3* doesn't officially cite *Detective Story 1* or *2*

as inspiration in any way, shape, or form,

then it's disqualified.


Also, to keep things simple,

I'll be specifically tracing the history

of the detective character, not mysteries in general.

There are certain moments we'll come across later,

but for the most part, this should help stabilize things.

And direct adaptations don't count,

what follows must be a new and unique character.


Finally, just for the sake of transparency,

said character(s) must be the protagonist.

If we include that one teenage girl

who so happens to be Sherlock Holmes's descendant

and only appears in a single episode of a long-running TV show,

we'll be here all week.


And with all that out of the way,

let's go back in time to our starting point...

# THE ROOTS
# AND TRUNK

# EDGAR ALLEN POE (Author)



So, there is a bit of a debate on who truly pioneered

the first modern detective fiction story.

Some point to the works of English author Wilkie Collins

such as *The Woman in White* (1859) and *Moonstone* (1868).[1]

Other say Émile Gaboriau and his character Monsieur Lecoq,

star of the 1868 French novel of the same name.[2]


The earliest point I can find

(and the one we'll be focusing on for the sake of simplicity)

takes us all the way back to American author Edgar Allen Poe.


The year is 1841.


First published in April of this year in *Graham's Magazine*,

the story story, *The Murders in the Rue Morgue*,

marks the first appearance of our fictional French detective,

**C. Auguste Dupin**.


Here, a once wealthy but now humble Dupin

is a private sleuth away from the law

who is brilliant enough to place himself

in the mind of the culprit.


His adventures are told through his close friend,

an unnamed narrator whom Dupin met

while searching for the same book at an obscure library.


Dupin would star in 2 more stories:


*The Mystery of Marie Rogêt* (1842),

and *The Purloined Letter* (1844).


The character's motivation for solving mysteries

would vary between stories.[3]


Now, it's worth noting that,

at the time of Dupin's conception,

the English word *detective* had not quite been termed yet.


Instead, Poe described Dupin's ability

using what he called *ratiocination*,

using logic, reasoning and imagination to solve his cases.[4]


Many agree that Poe's character helped lay the foundation

of what is today known as the great detective archetype.[5]

# ARTHUR CONAN DOYLE (Author)



Yeah, you knew this one was coming.

Inspired by Edgar Allen Poe's detective character[1]
as well as Monsieur Lecoq[2]
and real-life surgeon and lecturer Joseph Bell[3]
(among many other possible influences),
Conan Doyle penned and published this year his first novel,
*A Study in Scarlet*, in *The Strand Magazine*.

This would mark the first appearance of his now iconic character,
the brilliant but eccentric British consulting detective
**Sherlock Holmes**.

A master of observation and deductive logic,
along with a knack for forensics and disguise,
Holmes, often followed and biographed
by his good friend Dr. John H. Watson,
solve various mysteries on the streets of London and beyond.

Now, the first two novels, in the series,

A *Study in Scarlet* (1887) and *The Sign of the Four* (1890),

weren't the most well received when initially published.

But with *The Adventures of Sherlock Holmes*,

an anthology of short stories published

between July 1891 and June 1892,

the character of Sherlock Holmes would rise to stardom,

popularizing many of the tropes

we now associate with detective fiction today.[4]

The character would canonically appear

in a total of four novels and 56 short stories,

the last of which, *The Case-Book of Sherlock Holmes*,

collected short stories published

between October 1921 and April 1927.

Many, *many*, **many** unofficial original works

have been penned by separate authors since then

(pitting the great detective against the likes

of Jack the Ripper, Bram Stoker's *Dracula*,

and a particular foil we'll meet in just a moment),

and even more adaptations

of the main canon have been produced,

(including noteworthy portrayals by the likes of actors

Robert Downey Jr., Benedict Cumberbatch and Henry Cavill).

And don't get me started on original stories

set in the Sherlock Holmes canon,

such as Nancy Springer's *Enola Holmes* series

(starring Holmes' younger sister)

and Brittany Cavallaro's *A Study in Charlotte*

(starring Holmes' modern descendant).

It reached the point where, in May 2012,

Guinness World Records named Sherlock Holmes

*the most portrayed literary human character in film and television history.*[5]

# THE BRANCHES

## (BIG AND SMALL)

# THE GOLDEN AGE BEGINS



And here's where things get interesting.


Stories of mystery solvers

weren't completely unheard of before Conan Doyle

(as any Wilkie Collins or *Monsieur Lecoq* fan will tell you),

but the immense popularity of his character

meant there were a lot of people reading his stories.


And what happens if people like a work of art?


Well, chances are, they'll imitate it.


Even back when Conan Doyle was alive

and still publishing new Holmes adventures,

there were those who were inspired to make something similar,

something they could call their own.


Some of these, you'll find, were quite local,

and as close as any family member.

Others sat at the opposite end of the globe,

on a small island just opening up to the rest of the world.

From here, things won't be so much a straight line
as they are branches on a tree.

Our first example of this is...

# E.W. HORNUNG (Author)

BRITAIN, 1898

Hey, did you know Conan Doyle had a brother-in-law?
Because I sure didn't.


Very much inspired by Holmes[1] (and many other influences),
Ernest William Hornung decided it was time
to create his own character.


This character would have all the same skills as Holmes,
and would be known to the public as a prestigious cricketer.
But whereas Holmes was the hero,
this character would be the inverse:


A criminal.


Along with his own personal Watson,
Harry "Bunny" Manders,
**Arthur J. Raffles** (or, more commonly, A.J. Raffles)
would perform brilliant burglaries across London and beyond
as a so-called *gentleman thief*.[2]

Starting with *The Ides of March* in June 1898,

Raffles would be featured in a series of short stories

concluding with the 1909 novel, *Mr. Justice Raffles*.


Like Holmes, Raffles would find his own good deal of success,

seeing popular media adaptations

in the likes of film, television, theater and radio,

well into the 21$^{st}$ century.

# MAURICE LEBLANC (Author)

FRANCE, 1905

The director of *Je sais tout* magazine
came to Leblanc with a commission:

Pen a story in the same likes
of Sherlock Holmes and A.J. Raffles.[1]

This would be realized on July 15,
with a short story marking the debut
of my personal favorite literary character,
Gentleman Thief **Arsène Lupin**.

Lupin is a master of disguise and trickery,
fooling the local authorities with his antics
as much as he does the audience,
and at times you wonder if the stories
are playing with more...*fantastical* elements.

Beginning with *The Arrest of Arsène Lupin*,
this character would be featured in 17 novels and 39 novellas
and appear in various original works by separate artists.

Lupin's adventures would see several adaptations and spinoffs from theater, television, film, and even comics.

As an aside,
Leblanc published several stories pitting his character Lupin against Conan Doyle's Sherlock Holmes,
starting with *Sherlock Holmes Arrives Too Late* on June 15th, 1906.

Conan Doyle, famously, DID **NOT** like this.[2]

And so, due to legal concerns,
Leblanc was forced to change his name to Herlock Sholmes.
(Clever, I know.)

Nowadays,
as both characters have *technically* fallen into public domain
(Conan Doyle's estate is still currently very protective of their character),[3]
some modern republications have reverted to the original name.

# G.K. CHESTERTON (Author)

BRITAIN, 1910

This is one entry I almost didn't include,

but as it showed its influence and inspired many after it,

I felt it needed to be featured.


On July 23 of this year,

the short mystery story, *The Blue Cross*,

was published in *The Saturday Evening Post* by Chesterton,

marking the first appearance of his popular character,

Catholic priest and amateur detective **Father Brown**.


Father Brown is a very short and unassuming man who,

while easily blending into the background

of any given crime scene,

regularly solves mysteries with philosophy and psychology

rather than hard science and forensics[1]

(as Sherlock Holmes was known to do).


Now, Gilbert Keith Chesterton was many things:


An Author

A Poet

A Philosopher

A Christian Apologist[2]

Depending on what circle(s) you're in,

you may know his name for that last one.

However, for all his works in advocating Catholicism,

he's also strived in the world of detective fiction.

As an artist,

he was commissioned to illustrate 19 images

for an edition of Sherlock Holmes

that would, sadly, never see publication

(though these illustrations are officially available

thanks to G.K. *Chesterton's Sherlock Holmes,*

a collection edited together in 2003 by Steven Doyle).

Inspired by Holmes

and real-life Catholic priest John O'Conner

(who would later aid Chesterton's own conversion to Catholicism),[3]

he would create the character Father Brown

to reflect his own worldview.[4]

Father Brown would go on to appear in 53 short stories

between 1910 and the author's passing in 1936,
seeing success in adaptations in film, radio and television
throughout the 20th century.[4]

# AGATHA CHRISTIE (Author)



Strap yourselves in, folks, this one's a doozy!

Young Christie had long loved detective fiction of the time
from Sherlock Holmes to the works of Wilkie Collins.

With these influences,
she would publish this year her first story,
a detective novel titled *The Mysterious Affair at Styles*,
debuting the first of two of her iconic characters,
Belgian private investigator **Hercule Poirot**.

Like Holmes, Poirot is an eccentric
that you could easily write off as some silly foreigner in England,
but rest assured, as a former policeman, he's the best there is.

Christie's other iconic detective character, **Miss Jane Marple**,
is an elderly spinster solving mysteries
in the quaint English village of St. Mary Mead,
surprising anyone who may write her off

as some little old lady with no experience.

Miss Marple first debuted in the short story *The Tuesday Night Club*
(written after Christie was exhausted of Poirot),[1]
and was published in *The Royal Magazine* in December 1927.

Christie would go on to **DOMINATE** this genre.

Out of a staggering 66 detective novels and 15 anthologies
published between 1916 and 1976,
Poirot would appear in 33 novels and at least 50 short stories.
Miss Marple would see 12 novels and at least 20 short stories.

Her books have sold between 2 and **4 BILLION** copies
(numbers only contested by the *Bible*
and the works of legendary English playwright William Shakespeare).[2]

Her bestselling mystery novel, *And Then There Were None* (1939),
sold over 100 million copies alone as of June 2024.[3]

For the sake of demonstration (and this is a gross oversimplification),
if we say that Poe drew the outline of the detective character
and Conan Doyle colored the character in,
then we could say Christie drew and colored the background,

developing the rules and conventions of the mysteries

such a detective would solve.


This would include strategically placing

*each* and *every* suspect, culprit, victim and piece of evidence

in the crime scene in such a plausible way

that the audience could actually solve it on their own.


There's a reason Christie is officially known

as the *Queen of Mystery*.

# EDOGAWA RANPO (Author)



Because the intended wordplay won't make sense otherwise,

I'll be rendering this specific name in Japanese order,

with the family name (Edogawa) first.


Taro Hirai spent his adolescence

in the Japanese Meiji era (1868-1912).


For those unfamiliar with Japanese history,

this was a period of great change and reform

for the small island nation.

The history of this time is actually very rich and involved,

and there's just no possible way I can do it justice here.


But to give you a very brief summary for context:


Between 1603-1867 (the Edo Period, under the Tokugawa shogunate),

Japan had just spent the past 265 years in strict isolation,

officially closed off from the rest of the world.


This came to an end in 1853,

after American Commodore Matthew C. Perry

showed up with a naval fleet and an ultimatum:


*Either trade with us or get vanquished.*[1]


Japan, still operating at an almost Medieval level,

had no choice but to open their borders to Western trade.


And soon after, with the rise and leadership of Emperor Meiji,

Japan saw major social,

economic,

militaristic,

technological,

and cultural reforms

to compete with the Western world.[2]


One of the biggest things Japan adopted at the time

was Western literature, including the works of:


Lewis Carroll

Hans Christian Andersen

Edgar Allen Poe

Arthur Conan Doyle

and Maurice Leblanc.

Some of these names may stick out to you.

Now, Hirai was a big fan of Poe,
and it's said he actually worked to translate Conan Doyle's works
into Japanese during his years at Waseda University.[3]

This all came to a head in January 1925.
Now working under the pseudonym Edogawa Ranpo
(points to you if you understand this phonetic pun),
he would publish the short detective story
*The Case of the Murder on D. Hill.*

This would mark the debut of the character **Kogoro Akechi,**
a Japanese private eye who may remind you
a bit of Sherlock Holmes in much more ways than one.

For clarity, Edogawa made his writing debut
with the 1923 mystery *The Two-Sen Copper Coin*
in *Shin Seinen* (or *New Youth*) magazine,
and while not the first Japanese author of mystery fiction,[4]
he did closely tie
what were then more Western detective fiction tropes
to the Japanese culture and aesthetics of the time.[5]

This is greatly evident with the character of Akechi,

who is effectively to Japan what Holmes is to the West

in terms of character and cultural impact.

He solves mysteries in the streets of Tokyo and beyond,

often collecting info through a group of young boys dubbed

the Boys Detective Club (inspired by Holmes's Baker Street Irregulars),

and facing off against the infamous phantom thief,

the Lupin-inspired Fiend with Twenty Faces.

It's worth noting here that,

though Japanese translation of Leblanc's works,

the term *kaitou* (literally *phantom thief*)

would be adopted over the previously used *gentleman thief*.

(For simplicity and due to personal preference,

this is the term I'll be using going forward.)

Edogawa would go on to pen more than 40 mystery novels

between 1923 and his death in 1965.

Akechi would feature in at least 13 novels and 8 short stories.

*The Boys Detective Club* would also get a chance to shine,

being featured in 26 juvenile mystery novels

and at least 8 short stories and novellas.

(For you fans of American juvenile mystery novels such as

Edward Stratemeyer's *The Hardy Boys* and Carolyn Keene's *Nancy Drew*,

this is basically their Japanese equivalent.)


Edogawa himself would pretty much become

the face of Japanese detective fiction,

even having the *Edogawa Ranpo Prize*,

an annual literary award for then unpublished mystery novels,

named in his honor.[6]

# THE LEAVES AND FRUITS

# INTO THE MODERN ERA



From this point forward, all bets are off.

With the combined success and influence
of all our past named creators,
with many of them residing in different counties around the world,
the playing field is now too saturated to trace out specific lines.

As such,
I'd like to take the rest of this experiment
to name different branches that,
with our given guidelines, still fit onto our tree.

Now, just because I named this segment *The Leaves and Fruits*,
that in no way means these works had any less impact
than those that came before it.
In fact, you'll find many of these were smash hits
that changed the playing field for years and years to come.

With all this said and done,
let's start off with a dear friend of Edogawa Ranpo...

# SEISHI YOKOMIZO (Author)

JAPAN, 1946

Like many on our tree,

Yokomizo grew up reading various detective stories,

leading to him publishing his first story in 1921

in the magazine *Shin Seinen.*

This magazine had published the works

of several detective fiction authors before him,

including:

Edgar Allen Poe

Arthur Conan Doyle

G.K. Chesterton

and Edogawa Ranpo.

Edogawa was actually the first major Japanese writer

of detective fiction to be featured in the magazine,

and he regularly edited Yokomizo's works.

He even encouraged Yokomizo to move to Tokyo,

where, in 1946,

he would go on to publish a mystery novel titled *The Honjin Murders*,

starring the now iconic Japanese private eye **Kosuke Kindaichi**,

who you'll find excels with locked-room murder mysteries.

Kindaichi would go on to star in a total of 77 novels

between 1946 and Yokomizo's death in 1981,

his adventures selling over 55 million copies[1]

and seeing many adaptations across Japan,

from theater to television.

Again, for the sake of demonstration,

if we were to consider Edogawa the Conan Doyle of Japan,

then one could argue that Yokomizo was the Christie of Japan

with his mastery of locked-room setups.

And much like Edogawa,

Yokomizo has inspired the annual Japanese *Yokomizo Seishi Prize*,

awarded to then unpublished mystery novels.[2]

# MONKEY PUNCH (Manga Artist)



While you may snicker at Kazuhiko Kato's pseudonym,
the legacy of his work is nothing to sneeze at.

Imagine, if you will, that Arsène Lupin had a son,
who would take up the mantle of a phantom thief
just as his father did.

Now, imagine if said son
were to father a child of his own
with a Japanese woman.

Now, what would we name
this third incarnation of the Arsène Lupin legacy?

Arsène Lupin the Third?

Or, simply, **Lupin III**?

Yep, debuting in *Weekly Manga Action* on August 10, 1967,
Lupin III can best be described as the grandson of Arsène Lupin

with a dash of James Bond,

travelling the world as a renowned phantom thief and Casanova.


He's often accompanied by smooth sharpshooter Daisuke Jigen

(known for his 0.3-second quick-draw and superhuman accuracy)

and renegade samurai Goemon Ishikawa XIII

(thirteenth descendant of the real-life figure of the same name

—a Japanese Robin Hood of sorts)[1]

who wields the blade Zantetsuken (or *iron-cutting sword*),

sharp enough to slice through (quite literally) *anything* and *everything*.


Always one step behind the gang is Inspector Koichi Zenigata,

an older Interpol agent who,

with hand-to-hand combat prowess and a pair of handcuffs on a rope,

can best pretty much any other criminal he crosses

(save for Lupin, of course).


And finally, we have our regular femme fatale,

Lupin's on-again, off-again flame, Fujiko Mine.

As a very skilled thief of her own, she's not afraid to play sides,

whether it means using Lupin, Zenigata,

or anyone else to get what she wants.

(Fans of DC's *Batman* comics can compare her to the character Catwoman.)

These five characters I just described to you?

Yeah, that's quite literally **everything you need to know**
to jump into the series **at any point**,
be it the original manga,
any episode of the TMS animated series,
the TV specials, video games or film adaptations.

Much like Hanna-Barbera's popular *Scooby-Doo* franchise,
Lupin III thrives on its simplicity, timelessness, and ability
to throw the characters into almost any imaginable situation.

In fact, Lupin III would cross his own versions of characters
we previously met on our tree,
including Sherlock Holmes III,
an older and retired Kogoro Akechi,
and one Kosuke Kindani (based on Kosuke Kindaichi
—reading this now, I'm pretty sure it's a play on Japanese kanji).

And much like *Scooby-Doo*,
they saw a **wild** amount of success and adaptations
that continues well into the 21$^{st}$ century,
to the point where it inspired many outside the genre.

The 1979 animated film *The Castle of Cagliostro?*

Not only did it mark the directorial debut
of Studio Ghibli co-founder Hayao Miyazaki
(known for such films as *My Neighbor Totoro,*
*Kiki's Delivery Service* and *Spirited Away*),[2]
but it also inspired Pixar co-founder John Lasseter
(known later for work on *Toy Story, Monsters Inc.* and *Finding Nemo*),
who saw the film shortly after its release.[3]

# COLUMBO (TV Series)



This series has several co-creators:

writing duo Richard Levinson and William Link,

along with an iconic portrayal by actor Peter Falk.


Most mysteries, we find, focus on the point of view of the detective.

We follow them as they come across the mystery,

slowly gather the clues and eventually uncover the true culprit.


But what if it were the contrary?


What if we instead focused on the culprit?


No, not like Raffles or Lupin.

I mean, in a mystery setup you'd expect from Christie or Yokomizo,

what if we instead followed the perspective of the culprit

as they committed the crime and,

while being pursued by the detective,

manipulated evidence and conceived false alibis?


A sort of *inverted detective story*, if you will?

With this idea in mind and partially inspired by *Father Brown*,[1]
Levinson and Link would develop their famous character,
homicide detective **Lieutenant Columbo**.

Columbo has what you may call
a rather unimposing appearance:

Short stature
Dirty coat
Messy hair
Glass eye

All features of his actor, Peter Falk, if you can believe it.

In a similar vein to Miss Marple, however,
he will actively use this to his advantage.
Columbo himself is not a particularly violent man
(to the point where he, despite his position, almost never carries a gun),
it's just that the culprit tends to let their guard down around him.

After two pilot films in February 1968 and March 1971,
Columbo finally aired its first official episode, *Murder by the Book*
(directed by then newcomer Steven Spielberg, believe it or not),[2]

in September 1971.

The show would air new episodes
on a near monthly basis between 1971 and 1978,
and after a bit of a hiatus,
would air less frequently between 1989 and 2003.
(Japan initially listed these latter episodes under the title *New Columbo*.)[3]

Columbo would go on to become an icon
of detective fiction and televised crime dramas,
popularizing the inverted detective story format
and modernizing the idea of a police detective
who seems almost unqualified on the surface
showing why he holds his high status.

In fact, this character has even inspired the development
of *The Columbo Approach* or *The Columbo Method*,
where you bring up the contradictions to your client,
forcing them to doubt themselves and then asking them to clarify.[4]

This approach has been practiced across many fields,
from law enforcement to counseling
and even simple job interviews.

# GOSHO AOYAMA (Manga Artist)



Oh, my golly, where do I even start with you?

Like Christie, Aoyama has not one,
but (at least) *two* iconic characters,
each inspired by different branches on our tree.
Both saw publication in *Weekly Shonen Sunday* magazine.

Let's go in chronological order, shall we?
Starting in 1987…

Taking after his late father,
teenage Kaito Kuroba is a prodigy stage magician.
So brilliant, in fact,
that his illusions almost make you question your own reality.

At first, he's led to believe his father died due to a failed magic trick.
But he soon learns that there's more than meets the eye.

As it turns out,
his father was the infamous phantom thief **Kaitou Kid**

(yes, there is Japanese wordplay here),

and he was trying to stop a corrupt organization

from finding the Pandora Gem,

said to grant immortality to whoever drinks the tear it sheds.


Choosing to dawn the mantle as the second Kaitou Kid,

Kaito uses his magician skills

to make a name for himself as a great phantom thief

and find Pandora before anyone else.


Aoyama had long been a fan of phantom thieves

such as Arsène Lupin and Lupin III[1]

and, after publishing his first short story earlier that year,

decided to make his own phantom thief character.[2]

(Kid's costume is even an all-white version of Arsène Lupin's iconic outfit.)


And thus,

after writing, illustrating and publishing

a prototype short story titled *Nonchalant Lupin*,

the first chapter of *Magic Kaito* was published

on June 10, 1987.


Now, as popular as this series is,

it has a very...sporadic schedule.

As of June 2024,

the series has only seen 35 chapters collected into 5 volumes

between April 1988[3] and April 2024.[4]

(The series was actually updated less than 2 weeks ago as of writing this

with the 3-part story *Green Dragon*,

which has yet to be published in volume form.)


On paper, the series is currently still running to this day.


So why the weird schedule?


Well...things will really pick up for Aoyama in a moment.

For now, how about a quick detour?

# THE KINDAICHI CASE FILES (Manga Series)



Just like *Columbo*, this series has several co-creators:

Yozaburo Kanari and Seimaru Amagi as writers,

and Fumiya Sato as illustrator.

We already saw once before with Arsène Lupin and Lupin III

the idea of one character on this tree grandfathering another.

Lupin III teased us with Sherlock Holmes III,

but what about someone else?

How about...Kosuke Kindaichi?

Yes, our protagonist, **Hajime Kindaichi,**

may be the grandson of the legendary detective,

but he can be a bit of an unmotivated slacker at times.

Don't let this fool you, however.

He's just as brilliant as his grandfather,

and if you put him in the center of a locked-room murder mystery,

you'll get to see him truly shine.

*The Kindaichi Case Files* was first published

in *Weekly Shonen Magazine* on October 28, 1992,

eventually switching to *Evening* magazine starting January 23, 2018,[1]

later switching to the *Comic Days* manga app starting April 26, 2023[2]

(after *Evening* ceased production a few months prior in February)

where it continues to run to this day.


As of 2019, it has sold over 100 million copies.[3]


This series has seen many an adaptation,

from several animated and live action series,

to various light novels and video games.


One of these games in particular,

released for the Nintendo DS on February 5, 2009,

happened to cross over with...

# GOSHO AOYAMA (Manga Artist)



And so, we return to Aoyama.

Let's take a moment to set up the scene, shall we?

High schooler Shinichi Kudo is a prodigy detective,
brilliant enough to solve any case
you could possibly throw at him.

He's the son of a best-selling mystery author and a famous actress
(both currently abroad on business),
and is also a massive Sherlock Holmes fanatic
who can give you an endless list of fun facts
about Conan Doyle's stories and characters.

Now, while hanging out with his closest friend,
Ran Mouri, at the local amusement park,
he notices some men in black doing shady business
and decides to slip away and investigate.

One of these men sneaks up behind Shinichi and knocks him out,

opting to kill him with an untested experimental poison
said to be completely untraceable.

The poison doesn't kill him, however,
and when he finally does wake up,
his body has shrunken back down
to that of a roughly 7-year-old boy!

Thankfully, he manages to make it back home
and find a good family friend,
gadgeteer and inventor Professor Hiroshi Agasa.

After a change of clothes (they didn't shrink with his body, of course),
he explains everything to the Professor,
who decides that it's too dangerous
for Shinichi to reveal his identity to anyone else,
fearing the men in black will target him and anyone close to him.

At this exact moment,
Ran, worried about Shinichi's sudden disappearance,
shows up at Shinichi's home to see if he came by.

In a panic, Shinichi dawns an old pair of his dad's glasses,
and scrambling for a name,

he sees the works of Conan Doyle and Edogawa
sitting on the bookshelf behind him.

Conan...Edogawa...?

That's it!

And with that, he adopts the name **Conan Edogawa**
(he explains the English given name as being half British),
solving his usual mysteries around Beika City and beyond,
all while keeping his true identity secret,
investigating the *Black Organization* (the men in black),
and finding a way to return his body to normal.

(You can picture this series as Donald J. Sobol's *Encyclopedia Brown*
if much of his caseload was homicides.)

*Detective Conan* (known here in the English-speaking world as *Case Closed*)
first saw publication in *Weekly Shonen Sunday* magazine
on January 19, 1994.
New chapters continue running weekly as of May 2024.

Shortly following it was an anime adaptation,
which aired its first episode on January 8, 1996

and also continues into today.

To say this series is successful would very much be underselling it.

The manga hit its 1,100[th] chapter on September 28, 2022
and has sold over 270 million volumes as of January 2023.[1]
The anime aired its 1,000[th] episode on March 6, 2021.

Both have been critically acclaimed[2] for creating characters
on par with Conan Doyle and Edogawa,
while also creating plausible mysteries
on par with Christie and Yokomizo.

In fact, it's not uncommon to find references
to past entries of our tree all over the series
(Conan Edogawa is self-explanatory,
but the series is set in the fictional Beika City (Baker Street)
where one can find a Café Poirot and a Café Columbo,
Ran's father is a private investigator named Kogoro,
Professor Agasa's name is a Japanese rendition of Agatha,
and it goes on from there.)

By the way, remember Kaitou Kid from earlier?

Yep, he ended up migrating from *Magic Kaito*

and joining the cast of *Detective Conan* as a reoccurring rival!


...Actually, Kid quickly proved to be more popular

as a secondary character in this separate series

rather than as the protagonist of his own series.


(Go figure.)


Speaking of phantom thieves,

since the two series' respective animated adaptations

are both produced by TMS Entertainment,

Conan got to cross over with Lupin III at least twice:


Once in a televised special released in March 2009,

and again for a full length movie in December 2013.


And that's not all.


You see, *Weekly Shonen Sunday* and *Weekly Shonen Magazine*

(owned by publishing conglomerates Shogakukan and Kodansha respectfully)

both got their starts in March of 1959.


And what better way to celebrate a 50th anniversary

than by crossing over two of your most popular series?

Yes, from April to September of 2008,
*Detective Conan* teamed up with *The Kindaichi Case Files*
for a series of 12 magazine specials released biweekly.[3]

And (as mentioned earlier),
they would also see a Nintendo DS video game crossover
in February of 2009.[4]

Pretty crazy stuff if you ask me.

# ACE ATTORNEY (Video Game Series)



Now, this franchise is a product

of very heavy (but just as clever) localization.

As such, I will be referring to the series and characters

by their English names for the sake of convenience.

(Don't worry, I'll be sure to note the original Japanese names when necessary.)

Let's take a trip to the year 2016.

Rookie defense attorney **Phoenix Wright** (Ryuichi Naruhodo)

had just joined the small but successful Fey & Co. Law Offices,

training under its founder, Mia Fey (Chihiro Ayasato).

Having reached a swift acquittal in his first official trial,

it seems everything is going swimmingly...

...until Mia is found murdered in her office a month later.

(Well then.)

What's worse, her younger sister,

spirit medium Maya Fey (Mayoi Ayasato),

is the prime suspect.

Knowing what it's like to be alone in the world,

Phoenix takes it upon himself to clear her name

and uncover the true culprit.

Once succeeding, Maya joins Phoenix as his assistant,

and, having inherited the law firm from his late mentor,

they team up to form Wright & Co. Law Offices!

As an agency, they take on a variety of clients

from good friends to TV personalities,

and face off against many unique prosecutors,

from a famous rock star with his own band

to a convicted felon on death row.

In these trials, don't expect any less than a turnabout.

Created by Shu Takumi and published by Capcom,

the first game in this visual novel adventure series

would be released in Japan as *Gyakuten Saiban* (or *Turnabout Trial*)

on the Game Boy Advance on October 12, 2001.

It would eventually see a remaster for the Nintendo DS
on September 15, 2005,
which would be localized and released in North America
later that year on October 11
as *Phoenix Wright: Ace Attorney.*

As of June 2024, the series has seen six mainlines games
(all currently collected into two remastered trilogies),
as well as two spinoff games
starring Phoenix's prosecutor rival, Miles Edgeworth (Reiji Mitsurugi),
and two prequel games
starring Phoenix's ancestor, Ryonosuke Naruhodo.
(This character actually travels to Victorian London
and teams up with Sherlock Holmes,
known in the English localization as Herlock Sholmes.)

The *Ace Attorney* series has seen critical success,
selling over 11 million copies worldwide as of May 2024,[1]
and being adapted into manga, an animated TV series,
a live action film, and even a stage show.

Takumi cites many inspirations for the *Ace Attorney* series.

He recalls his own childhood experiences for Phoenix's backstory (though, unlike Phoenix, Takumi's own personal story didn't end like so),[2]

Edogawa Ranpo's short story *The Psychological Test*,

where the criminal spins a testimony full of contradictions,[3]

*Columbo* for its inverted detective story format

(which marks the first case in each *Ace Attorney* game),[4]

and the American legal drama series *Perry Mason*,

starring a Los Angeles defense attorney

who operates very much like Phoenix Wright.[5]


...Oh, that's right!

This series also received a crossover game in November of 2012.


And that crossover was with...

# PROFESSOR LAYTON (Video Game Series)



Imagine, what would happen

if we combined Sherlock Holmes with Indiana Jones?


Our next entry takes us to the city of London.


Employed at Gressenheller University

as an archeology professor

is one **Hershel Layton**.


Now, Layton happens to have a strong passion for puzzles.

And a talent.

Like, a world-renowned talent.


This often leads Layton,

as well as his adolescent (self-proclaimed) apprentice Luke Triton,

on adventures across the city and the world,

from a box that supposedly kills whoever opens it

to a specter terrorizing a small mountain village

or even a time machine demonstration gone wrong.

Created by Akihiro Hino and published by Level-5,

the first title in this puzzle adventure series,

*Professor Layton and the Curious Village*,

released for the Nintendo DS in Japan on February 15, 2007,

releasing internationally on February 10, 2008.

The series would go to spawn seven mainline titles

(soon to be eight with *Professor Layton and the New World of Steam*)

and a spinoff game starring one of Layton's children.

And, believe me, they've been a hit.

Over 18 million copies sold worldwide as of June 2024.[1]

Several manga and novel adaptations.

An animated film and TV series.

And remember how I said *Ace Attorney* had a crossover game?

That's right, Professor Layton and Phoenix Wright

would team up for a Nintendo 3DS adventure

on November 29, 2012 in Japan,

and later in 2014 internationally.

In fact, Hino has cited *Ace Attorney* as a partial influence, having heavily analyzed the character of Phoenix Wright

and working to amplify any good points

and improve any bad points

to create the character of Professor Layton.[2]


He was also inspired by *Atama no Taisou* (or *Head Gymnastics*),

a series of puzzle books created by Japanese psychologist Akira Tago,

which Hino enjoyed as a child.

Tago would also go on to personally design the puzzles

found in the *Professor Layton* series before his passing in 2016.[3]


From looking up to your heroes to working with them.


I think that's kinda neat.

# LUTHER (TV Series)



Well, we spent quite a bit of time in Japan,
but how about we finally return to Europe?

For himself and those close to him,
Detective Chief Inspector **John Luther**
is a little too dedicated to his job,
able to delve deep into the darkness
without being consumed himself.

He's a legend in his field,
able to pursue one conniving criminal after another.

...Well, save for genius psychopathic criminal Alice Morgan,
who not even Luther can find the evidence to convict,
despite knowing full well she's responsible.

Though ultimately Luther's archenemy,
Morgan does often use her unique criminal insight
to aid Luther in catching criminals
while not being convicted himself.

Created by British writer Neil Cross

and portrayed by actor Idris Elba,

*Luther* ran for 20 episodes spread across 5 seasons

between May 2010 and January 2019,

with a film continuation, *Luther: The Fallen Sun,*

releasing in 2023.


The series has seen critical acclaim internationally,

and according to creator Neil Cross,

Luther is said to have the intellect of Holmes

while using the criminal's perspective à la Columbo.[1]


As weird as it sounds,

I feel my thoughts are best given

in the *Spotlight Corner Extravaganza* section of this book.


I invite you to take a look at it when you get the chance.

# KNIVES OUT (Film Series)



...Wait, what!? A new entry??
This wasn't in the original release!

Yep, those of you who read
the original 2023 version of *The Detective's Journey*
will tell you this is new.

Honestly, I can't believe I glossed over it before.

Hailing from the southern US
(as you can tell by his...deep discernible accent)
is private eye **Benoit Blanc** (portrayed by *James Bond* himself Daniel Craig),
often considered the world's greatest detective.

In the first film, *Knives Out,*
Blanc is invited to a mansion in Massachusetts,
where best-selling mystery author Harlan Thrombey
(played by the late Christopher Plummer)
was found dead after his 85$^{th}$ birthday party.
A party attended by members of his entire family,

many of whom he either had a rocky relationship with

or were using good graces to wind up in his will.


In the 2022 sequel, *Glass Onion*

(notably shot and set during the 2020 COVID-19 pandemic),

tech tycoon Miles Bron (played by actor Edward Norton)

invites his friends (all successful and influential people)

to his mansion on a private island in Greece.

The mansion's name? The Glass Onion.

Blanc himself also seems to have gotten an invitation,

despite the fact Bron never sent him one...


The *Knives Out* films

were written, produced and directed

by one Rian Johnson.


Now, if that name sounds familiar,

you might have seen one or more of his other films,

such as *Break* (2005), *Looper* (2012),

or (as much as *Star Wars* fans might disown it) *The Last Jedi* (2017).

(Apparently, he also directed the episodes

*Fly*, *Fifty-One* and *Ozymandias* of the hit AMC show *Breaking Bad*,

because I know someone will want me to mention it.)

Johnson grew up on the works of Agatha Christie

and had long wanted to create his own kind of whodunnit,

with the original idea for *Knives Out*

being conceived around the time he made *Break*.[1]


The problem?

Well, putting aside the time and resources

(it was mainly thanks to his work on *The Last Jedi* that he got the chance at all),

studios and even some audiences

saw the idea of a typical whodunnit kinda...well, outdated.[2]

(While I say this whole tree is evidence of that not being entirely true,

I do understand the sentiment.)


Johnson knew he had to modernize it.

Play with the formula, create new archetypes.


He relied on Alfred Hitchcock

and his views on plot development in such stories.[3]

As much internet backlash as he got from *The Last Jedi*,

the film was a major coping mechanism for him,

even inspiring elements of the story and characters.[4]


And...as much as I'm allergic to politics,

you can't deny that the film does scrutinize

various elements of our modern American society.[5]

All that work paid off in the end.

The first film released to critical acclaim,
grossing $312.9 million[6] against a $40 million budget.[7]
The second film did similarly well,
though you could say it was somewhat hindered
by releasing on Netflix during the pandemic.[8]
And it was announced in 2023
that a third film, *Wake Up Dead Man*, is set for release in 2025.[9]

Also, did I mention each of these films has an all-star cast?
Because I think that's a fun and clever way
to subvert the *big-name celebrity is the victim and/or culprit* trope.
(I say *and/or* because, well, you really don't know with these whodunnits.)

# LUPIN (TV Series)

FRANCE, 2021

And finally, let's wrap things up with a trip to France.


**Assane Diop** is a professional thief
whose father, 25 years prior,
was framed by the rich and powerful Hubert Pellegrini
for stealing a priceless diamond necklace.


This would end up resulting in his arrest
and later his supposed death in prison.


Shortly after his arrest, however,
he gave his son Assane a novel,
the original stories of *Arsène Lupin, Gentleman Burglar*.


Assane, inspired by the character in the present day,
would style himself after the titular phantom thief
and use his mastery of disguise and thievery,
as well as his charisma to get revenge on Pellegrini.


Created by George Kay and François Uzan

and portrayed by actor Omar Sy,

*Lupin* would premiere the first part of its first season

on January 8, 2021,

and the second part later that year on June 11.


With 76 million viewers in its first month,[1]

it became Netflix's most watched non-English show of the time[2]

(later surpassed by *Squid Game* in September of 2021,

with 142 million viewers in its first four weeks).[3]


Much like *Luther*,

my thoughts are better demonstrated

in the *Spotlight Corner Extravaganza* section.


Go ahead, you might be as surprised as I was.

# INDIGO

# SPEAKEASY

## A CONCLUSION & INVITATION

# ···ONE TRUTH PREVAILS!

w/ SS REED

And with that, our journey comes to a close.


It's been an interesting ride, hasn't it?
We've travelled all around the world and back:


America

Britain

France

Japan


From North America to Europe and even East Asia,
all across the span of nearly 2 centuries.


We've seen the birth of the modern great detective,
how people built on the concept and made it their own.
Some took the idea and refined it,
while others reshaped it into something new.


We've even seen how people
of different times, cultures and backgrounds

may work with the same, already established idea.

I had a lot of fun doing research on this project,
and it taught me about the history of one of my favorite genres.
It let me reanalyze stories and characters I already love,
and it introduced me to new ones that I can now enjoy.

I actually encourage you reading this
to form your own tree of inspiration.

Pick a genre, trope or character archetype that you personally enjoy.
It could be foreign, or it could be local.
It could be niche or mainstream, classic or modern.
There's no limit to your choice.

Now, taking into account the rules I listed in the beginning
(or making your own rules if you feel you can flow better),
try to go back as far as you possibly can
to what you think is the earliest modern appearance of your topic.

After that, just outline the tree.

You may find that your research on a big branch
may itself lead you to a particular small branch.

Maybe you have a story or character in mind
that you think could work as a small branch,
but your research shows it's actually a big branch
that connects to the base.

Some entries you may have been certain of
before the tree is even formed.
Others, you'll find, are new to your world
and expand the tree evermore.

And, once your tree is finished,
whether it looks similar to mine or completely different,
how about sharing it with us on social media!
(Links will be listed in the back of this book.)

Finally, take a moment, really ask yourself...

...what was your takeaway from all of this?

Curious about these creators,

stories and characters

that have inspired me?

# SPOTLIGHT CORNER

# EXTRAVAGANZA

Today's featured guests···

# GREAT DETECTIVES & PHANTOM THIEVES

THE WHERE, WHY & HOW

So...this *Spotlight Corner* is gonna be

a little different from what we've done before.

In every other version,

we only focus on one story, character or creator at a time.

But, because of the nature of this essay

(really, this book as a whole),

that's not so easy.

The Great Detective (and, by extension, the Phantom Thief)

is and has been one of,

if not my favorite character archetype in fiction.

(Only the superhero and mad scientist can compete.)

Some of these are stories and characters

I've been in love with since I was a child or teenager,

while others sparked my interest for the first time

while working on this piece.

And I'm sure the same can be said for you, my dear reader.

Is there a story here you know well

and would like to reconnect with?

Is there a fresh story here that tickles your fancy

and you'd like to experience it yourself?

This *Spotlight Corner* will be dedicated to showing you

where you can officially (and legally) find each of these stories,

why you might enjoy each story (including my own personal experiences),

and how best to enjoy each story.

Now, for a bit of pretense,

I am mostly approaching this from the perspective

of an English-speaking American.

For those of you translating or localizing this work

(or simply updating it for contemporary editions),

I trust you to make the proper adjustments.

It's a *Spotlight Corner Extravaganza*, baby!

(All of these are up to date as of June 2024).

### C. AUGUSTE DUPIN

In an interesting twist,

I owned all three of these stories

and didn't know it until working on this piece.


I own a copy of Canterbury Classics' *Selected Works of Edgar Allen Poe.*

While I'm not personally a fan of the author,

I did want to see how one man spent his life

spinning short stories for profit in a time when it wasn't easy to.

(Though, I will admit, I can see why *The Tell-Tale Heart* is so beloved.)


When I started writing this piece,

these stories interested me,

so I spent a good deal of time

searching my local bookstore and library,

expecting to find a novella collection of sorts.


No dice.


Once I saw my Poe collection on the shelf,

a lightbulb went off in my mind,

and sure enough,

all 3 stories were available in full.


These stories are an interesting read,

not just comparing them to later works
like those of Conan Doyle and Christie,
but just on their own, as the stories of a French detective.

I will warn you, though, that these stories were written
before the modern rules of detective fiction were really established,
so those of you trying to solve the mysteries with those rules in mind
may raise a few question marks.

...There's not much to recommend here besides the original stories.
You can read them wherever books are sold.
Audiobooks are also available.

## SHERLOCK HOLMES

I think it was around my late teens or early 20s when I received
a copy of *The Complete Sherlock Holmes* collection for Christmas,
but the character has been on and off my radar
for as long as I can remember.

Before that, I was immersed in so many other detective stories:

*Detective Conan*
*Ace Attorney*

*Professor Layton*


I had even found a copy of *The Hound of the Baskervilles*
in my high school library.
(While I did first pick up the story here, I didn't get far into it at that point.)


The detective character has always fascinated me since childhood,
and many of them always referenced Holmes in one way or another.


When I finally got the chance to read the original stories myself,
I was surprised.


See, there's a lot of tropes associated with Holmes today
that hold little to no significance in the original stories:


The phrase *elementary, my dear Watson*
is written at no point on any page of any story,
his iconic deerstalker cap was a product of Sidney Paget
and his original illustrations for *The Boscombe Valley Mystery*
rather than Conan Doyle's own texts,
and Watson was in no way some chubby dullard.


Reading the stories,
filtering out the stereotypes of Holmes and his world,

almost makes them as fresh as any contemporary bestseller.

When I first started publishing my own fiction works,
I tried to create my own detective character of this caliber.
That original attempt was canned long ago,
not to say I haven't toyed with the idea in recent years.

The Sherlock Holmes stories are so plentiful
that I don't need to tell you where to find them,
be they print editions or audiobooks.

I personally like to read stories in the order the author intends,
which is often in publication order.
In that case, start with *A Study in Scarlet*.

My personal favorite story is *A Scandal in Bohemia*,
which sees Holmes face off against Irene Adler,
but if you want something more novel length
and you don't care much for chronology,
*The Hound of the Baskervilles* is a good start.

### A.J. RAFFLES

If I can be perfectly honest,

I did not know this character existed until working on this piece,
and it's the first title that, as of writing this,
I have not experienced myself.

As a fan of Sherlock Holmes and Arsène Lupin,
it was interesting seeing a character that meets in the middle,
especially with the author being the brother-in-law of Conan Doyle.

Like Dupin, the only way I can imagine
experiencing the original stories in chronological order.
And, yes, there are audiobook adaptations available.

## ARSÈNE LUPIN

Behold, my favorite literary character of all time!

Much like the detective,
the phantom thief is an archetype that has always been on my radar
for as long as I can remember.

My earliest exposure that I can recall
is probably the game *Rhythm Thief and the Empire's Treasure*,
published by Sega for the Nintendo 3DS in 2012.
(Great game, by the way. Play it if you can.)

After that, I encountered many thieves harping back to Lupin,
from Kaitou Kid to Lupin III.


...Actually, it would seem that Japan rather adores Lupin.
(Maybe even more so than his homeland.)


Throughout my teens,
the phantom thief was my favorite character type,
and I finally got to pick up a copy of the original stories
at my local bookstore in my early 20s.
(As of writing this, I own two copies:
a Penguin Classics edition which is being lent to a close relative,
and an illustrated edition by Vincent Mallié;
both switch between using Sherlock Holmes and Herlock Sholmes.)


Before and after reading Lupin's adventures,
I have never met a character so clever, so spellbinding, so...fun!


And yet...this character seems almost unheard of here in the states.


Bring up the name Arsène Lupin,
and you'll be lucky if you get someone
that thinks you're referencing Lupin III,

the French Netflix series *Lupin*,

or Atlus's hit role-playing game *Persona 5*.

(Though I've been a huge fan of the *Persona* series since the days of 3 and 4,

I do not consider this to be a phantom thief story at its absolute core,

but that's a conversation for another time.)


The adventures of Lupin

have been a key inspiration in how I craft my characters,

from how they're always more than meets the eye

to how they can steal the show when you least expect it.


I say start with the first collection, *Arsène Lupin, Gentleman Burglar*.

The first story? *The Arrest of Arsène Lupin*.

Perfect introduction to what kind of character he is.

## FATHER BROWN


When I started working on this piece,

this story was not on my radar.

Like, at all.


It was only when I started doing research,

and then I saw *Columbo* named it as an inspiration.

I didn't think much of it at the time,

but then I saw *Detective Conan* make a reference to it.


And then I saw that the author

was officially connected to *Sherlock Holmes*.


This was enough for me to look into the character,

and I didn't realize how much of an impact

this character has had in detective fiction.


All this said, I have yet to read these stories myself.


To my understanding,

Father Brown's biggest impact was the fact

that he was an unsuspecting man you wouldn't think twice about

if you met him at a crime scene.

Someone who wasn't a cop,

and ultimately was no threat to you as the culprit.


These qualities hiding a sharp mind

that could dissect your whole character in a heartbeat.


For those going chronologically, *The Blue Cross* is the way to go.
*The Secret Garden,*

*The Sins of Prince Sardine,*

*The Paradise of Thieves,*

and *The Sign of the Broken Sword* are popular, too.

## AGATHA CHRISTIE

For gripping mysteries you can actually solve,

Christie is the way to go.


Growing up, if people were talking mysteries

but weren't referencing Conan Doyle,

they were referencing Christie.


While I haven't personally read her books

(I picked up a copy of *Murder on the Orient Express*

from my high school library but barely opened it),

I have experienced her stories.


Even before my viewing of Kenneth Branagh's

2017 film adaptation of *Murder on the Orient Express*,

this is a story I often saw referenced growing up,

from Chapter 6 of *Paper Mario: The Thousand Year Door*

on the Nintendo Gamecube

(which actually released a Switch remake in May 2024)

to *Professor Layton and the Diabolical Box* on the Nintendo DS.

This story even acted as the framework
for my story *Eight Clouds Express*
before I further developed the setting and characters.

Now, for Christie's biggest bestseller,
*And Then There Were None* is a classic among classics.
It plays with the tropes of detective fiction to create a setting
where no character is safe, no character can be trusted.

As for Miss Marple, I can only recommend her first story,
*The Thirteen Problems*.

## EDOGAWA RANPO

Now, here's where things get tricky.

You see, as of writing this,
only a handful of Edogawa's works
have been officially translated into English.

My first exposure to the writer came from *Detective Conan*,
after the title character assumes Edogawa as his family name.

As such,

I can't say I have any personal experiences with these stories,

although I'd *really* like to.

Not only am I a fan of Sherlock Holmes,

but also Japanese culture and classic literature

(I own an English copy of Soseki Natsume's *I Am a Cat*,

and I have spent some time reading the Japanese *Kojiki*,

which records old Shinto myths).

The adventures of Kogoro Akechi tick both of these boxes.

For a standalone story, *The Two-Sen Copper Coin*

has been revered by critics for being a Victorian detective fiction story

set in Japan and starring Japanese characters.

...It's actually kinda hard for me to recommend anything for this one.

This part is mostly just me curiously pondering

on what these stories entail.

At the very least, I'm glad more companies and translators

are working to bring these stories to the West...

**SEISHI YOKOMIZO**

...which I guess is also the case for Yokomizo's works.

Translators and localizers are still working hard
to bring Kosuke Kindaichi's adventures to the West.
As of this essay,
Pushkin Vertigo has so far published 6 of his works:

*The Honjin Murders*
*The Inugami Curse*
*The Village of Eight Graves*
*Gokumon Island*
*The Devil's Flute Murders*
and *The Little Sparrow Murders*

Personally, I like a bit more variety in my mysteries
beyond just locked room murders,
but when spaced out properly, they can be exciting.

And from what I hear,
there's no better way to experience this
than with Kosuke Kindaichi.

For chronologically, I'd say start with *The Honjin Murders*.

Otherwise, *The Inugami Curse* is the way to go.

## LUPIN III

Now, for these past few entries,
I've been struggling with what to write down,
such as where to find each story and where to start.

Classic literature is a hard thing to track and recommend,
especially when you haven't read them yourself.

From here, though, this is where things start to get fun.

As I mentioned earlier,
*Lupin III* thrives on the fact that you can start at any series,
any time, any point, and you'll still be able to enjoy it.

The world really is your oyster here.

I got into *Lupin III* in my teens,
and it still stands in my personal top ten
of favorite anime series.

Much like his grandfather,

Lupin III prides himself as a phantom thief,
and has all the tricks and charm to pull it off.

But it's not all so serious,
these characters can be very self-aware
and know how to have fun with it.

The characters' antics often verges on *Looney Tunes* territory,
and Lupin's relationship with Zenigata
almost makes them a human *Tom and Jerry*.

In fact, it's this relationship that helped inspire *World's End Island*
(and the *Clover & Gold* series as a whole),
a short story in my *Eight Clouds Express* anthology.

Even the fact that Goemon's sword
can slice literally anything is a running gag.
(*"Once again, I have cut a worthless object."*)

My personal favorite title is *The Castle of Cagliostro*,
which is great if you want a story with a Ghibli touch.
For those of you who want a CG animated adventure,
check out *Lupin III: The First*.

I also remember liking *Blood Seal of the Eternal Mermaid*,

but last I checked, reception was mixed for some reason?

(I dunno, it's been a minute since I watched it.)


*The Mystery of Mamo* is also a worthy classic,

though I've yet to watch it myself.


I also think the original series is worth checking out,

but, like everything I name here,

that's really a case of *pick whatever interests you.*


While the original manga is good,

I'd say be careful if you start with it.

Not that it's bad in any sense,

but it's quite different

from the now almost family-friendly franchise

we know and love today.

(Not that *Lupin III* can't deal with more adult or mature elements,

as fans of *The Woman Called Fujiko Mine* and *Goemon's Blood Spray* can tell you.)


For those here in America,

TMS Entertainment and Discotek Media

have been working hard in recent years

to make the franchise readily available and accessible to the public.

Definitely give this one a shot!

## COLUMBO

Ah, Columbo. Such a dear series to me.

Despite spending my childhood in the 2000s,
I've always liked watching older shows.

*Star Trek*
(Often *The Original Series*, but I love *The Next Generation*.)
*Murder, She Wrote*
(Also created and produced by Levinson and Link, along with Peter S. Fischer.)
*Quantum Leap*
(Love the original series, but the 2022 reboot is good, too.)

My personal favorite of these,
and arguably my favorite TV show of all time,
is *Columbo*.

I always saw this series paired up
with the likes of other detective shows
like *Monk* (starring Tony Shalhoub) and *Murder, She Wrote*,

but *Columbo* in particular is the one that won my heart.


There's just something about a character
(especially detectives) that I like
where you never quite know what's going on in their head.


Columbo is a man of many quirks.
Not too many to seem like he's trying too hard,
but just enough to make you question
if he's worthy of his police badge.
(Believe me, he is.)


On one hand, you see him when he's alone,
and he acts no different from a lost dog.
On the other, he has admitted to occasionally
fabricating facts about himself and his personal life.
(It helps that actor Peter Falk adlibbed many of his own lines,
which regularly caught *the other actors* off guard.)


One of his most iconic bits is Columbo
talking to who the audience knows is the culprit,
only for him to leave without a shred of evidence or testimony...


...and immediately return,

excusing himself with *just one more thing,*

and pulling a level of sleuthing to the culprit

that would make Sherlock Holmes jealous.


Speaking of the culprit,

this series is why the inverted detective story

is my favorite format in detective fiction.

There's a deep intimacy, focusing on the culprit

as he's slowly backed into a corner,

all while you try to predict what his next move will be.

(My second favorite example of this is the manga and anime *Death Note,*

as Light Yagami battles L to see who can unmask the other first

in an epic game of cat and mouse.)


In a normal mystery,

it's the same feeling as the detective waiting

for the culprit to strike again.


(It's invigorating!)


*Columbo,* as a series, isn't just an episodic journey,

but each episode stands alone as a full length made-for-TV movie.

Meaning that, across its 30+ year run,

you can jump in at any point,

watch the episodes in any order,

and still be satisfied.


The first episode I ever watched was *Murder, Smoke and Shadows,*

with the culprit being a boy genius Hollywood director.

One thing you'll notice throughout the series is that each culprit,

in one way or another, is a member of high society.


Doctors

Celebrities

Politicians

CEOs


The sky's the limit.


While I still praise the episode today,

the episode with my favorite culprit is *A Stitch in Crime,*

with *Star Trek* actor Leonard Nimoy

playing cardiac surgeon Dr. Barry Mayfield.


After seeing him play a nearly emotionless

but otherwise goodhearted Spock,

it was terrifying (in the best way) seeing him play an antagonist

as cold and calculating with murder

as he would with open heart surgery

and mask it with more human emotions.


As a final recommendation,

I introduced my mother to the series

at the same time I discovered it.

I picked almost every episode to watch until that point,

so I decided to let her choose one for the night.


She landed on the episode *By Dawn's Early Light*.

The culprit? Colonel Lyle C. Rumford,

head of the all-boys Haynes Military Academy.

This episode really did feel like a 1970s detective film

in scope and writing.


*Columbo* has been a large influence

in how I deal with perspective in fiction.


And I hope you reading this can find a new perspective

when enjoying this series yourself.


## MAGIC KAITO


Gosho Aoyama has to be

my favorite manga artist in the industry today,

with an art style so unique and memorable,

and stories that always leave me coming back for more.


*Yaiba*

The adventures of a young samurai in modern Japan.

(This one's actually getting a new anime adaptation by Wit Studio.

Like, it was announced May 2024, not even a day or two as I'm writing this.)


*3ʳᵈ Base 4ᵗʰ*

A mediocre high school baseball player who buys a bat

that nets him a home run every time he uses it.

The catch? He has to pay out of pocket for each hit.


And these are just his works collected into full-length volumes.

He also has several short stories under his belt,

many of them collected into *Gosho Aoyama's Collection of Short Stories*:


*Wait a Minute*

A boy genius invents a time machine jetpack.

His love interest takes off with it and jumps two years into the future.


*Tell Me a Lie*

A high school girl who can read anyone's thoughts

when looking straight into their eyes.


*The Santa Claus of Summer*
A high school boy is dumped by his girlfriend.
After a curious string of events,
he accidently sets a weaponized satellite
to obliterate Earth within 24 hours.


*Play It Again*
After losing to his granddaughter in a sword fight,
an old man honors her wish not to visit her at school for parent day.
He rests underneath a cherry blossom, dreaming of his lost youth.
When he wakes up, he finds his dream has come true.


Aoyama's stories have always captivated me,
and *Magic Kaito* is no different.
If I could, I'd have these stories on my shelf,
worn down from being read over and over again.


Now, it's with a heavy heart that I say this,
but it can't be ignored.
You see, as of writing this segment,
the *Magic Kaito* manga, along with much of Aoyama's work...

...has never been officially published in the English language.

(A crime against humanity, if you ask me!)

Thankfully, there is a saving grace.

See, there are two animated adaptations out there.
The first was a series of TV specials
animated by TMS Entertainment
(the studio behind *Detective Conan* and *Lupin III*)
called *Magic Kaito: Kid the Phantom Thief*.

Personally, I feel this is the superior adaptation,
as they used what they learned from both series to make this.
However, this series also never saw an official English release,
so most of us are pretty much out of luck.

The other series is called *Magic Kaito 1412*,
and was produced by A-1 Pictures
(who also produced the first season of the *Ace Attorney* TV anime)
to celebrate *Detective Conan*'s 20-year manga anniversary.

While *Kid the Phantom Thief* stands alone as a *Magic Kaito* story,
with only small easter eggs to *Detective Conan* sprinkled in,

*1412* also goes as far as adapting Kid's various matchups
against Conan Edogawa
(as seen in *Detective Conan* from a flipped perspective),
making him a regular appearance in the show.

I'd say *Kid the Phantom Thief*
handle the premise and characters better,
but *1412* handles the setting and aesthetics better.

For any English-speaking Americans who are curious,
the latter series has been officially translated
and released by Crunchyroll.
Go check it out and tell them I said hi!

Now, the character of Kaitou Kid...

...is very important to me.

After *Rhythm Thief and the Empires Treasure,*
*Magic Kaito* was my first big exposure to phantom thieves,
even before *Lupin III.*

Even now,
Kaitou Kid stands as my all-time favorite manga/anime character.

His iconic white suit, his elaborate disguises,

his level of stage magic that almost seems to warp reality,

and he does it all with a solid poker face.


Even now, I find him charming in a way

that I can't say about many other characters.


On top of that,

with how series creator Gosho Aoyama

designed both Kaito Kuroba and Shinichi Kudo,

the resemblance between the two (both on paper and in-universe)

is almost uncanny.


Both characters are well aware of this,

and it's not uncommon for Kaito to disguise himself as Shinichi

(the only disguise he doesn't need full makeup and prosthetics for,

just the slightest change of hairstyle and speech patterns),

and Shinichi, as Conan trying to hide his true identity?

He can't say single a word as to not expose himself.


That said, it's heavily implied

they both know the other's true nature,

but out of mutual respect as worthy opponents,

they have a gentlemen's agreement

not to hunt each other down

unless one actively prompts the other.


Heck, they'll even go so far as teaming up

if the situation demands it.


Kaitou Kid has gone on to act as inspiration for my stories,

most notably the *Math Rock* story *A New Illusion*.


Seriously, if I meet you on the street

and you know who this character is,

we're friends, no questions asked.


## THE KINDAICHI CASE FILES


As I said previously,

I prefer more variety in my mysteries than just locked room murders.

But if you do it well, I will give you praise for it.


This is very much the case for *The Kindaichi Case Files*.


Back during high school,

I remember watching a few episodes of the 1997 anime series.

It ultimately didn't stick with me, but for what it's worth,
the mysteries are very well executed and thought out.

I do remember it being a tad formulaic,
with each culprit usually being treated as a tragic character
and trying to commit suicide out of guilt once caught.

That said, it's that similar *Nancy Drew/Hardy Boys* quality
that I feel is worth checking out.

*The Kindaichi Case Files* is a tricky series to follow in English.
Tokyopop did translate and publish
the first 17 volumes of the manga,
but they stopped back in July 2008.

None of the live action specials have been translated,
and while Crunchyroll did stream
*The File of Young Kindaichi Returns* during its initial airing,
it seems to no longer be available on the site.

If you really love mysteries,
I say give it a shot, if you can find it.

## DETECTIVE CONAN (or CASE CLOSED)

I think it was around middle school,
before I really got into manga, anime and light novels.

A friend of mine recommended me three titles:

*Shaman King* (the original anime, which I did enjoy)
*Blue Gender* (which I still haven't watched)
and *Detective Conan* (or *Case Closed* if you speak English)

When I entered high school
and really started exploring the medium of Japanese entertainment,
I made watching *Detective Conan* a priority.

When I ultimately stopped watching anime in July 2016,
the manga had over 960 chapters,
the anime over 820 episodes.

And having used my free time during high school (sorry, Mom),
I was fully caught up on both.

While there are stories out there
that hold a more special place in my heart,
I am by no means exaggerating when I say:

This is, without a shadow of a doubt,

my favorite anime/manga series of all time.

It greatly inspired what stories I tell and how I tell them.
(I think *The Melancholy of Haruhi Suzumiya* is the only series that competes
—funny enough, both title characters share the same English voice actress,
Wendee Lee.)

In fact, it's entirely the reason
why we have *Spotlight Corner* in the first place,
being inspired by *Gosho Aoyama's Detective Picture Book*,
where, at the end of each *Detective Conan* volume,
he highlights a different great detective
(or someone who can loosely be considered one) in fiction,
illustrating a special portrait for them,
saying where they're from
and even a personal recommendation of one of their stories.

He's covered detectives old and new,
popular and obscure, from the East and the West,
many of which actually appear as entries on our tree:

C. Auguste Dupin

Sherlock Holmes (the literary version and Benedict Cumberbatch's portrayal)

Arsène Lupin

Hercule Poirot

Miss Marple

Edogawa Ranpo

Inspector Zenigata (*Lupin III*)

Even (to my surprise) Professor Layton.

(Seriously, see for yourself

—he recommends more detective stories than I ever could.)


I could sit here all day gushing over the series,

but I'll try to keep it brief.


The series likes to keep its head in the clouds

and its feet on the ground.

While each individual mystery

is very well researched and quite plausible in reality

(I've heard Aoyama's older brother is a scientist who helps with the mysteries),

it also regularly juggles more fantastical elements

with the overall narrative and characters.


Of course, you have Conan (and later individuals such as Ai Haibara)

whose bodies were shrunken by the supposed poison,

but there are characters such as Ran Mouri and Makoto Kyogoku, karate masters who have shown enough prowess to,

on occasion,

PUNCH THROUGH *CONCRETE* AND DODGE **BULLETS**!


Conan also has a large variety of special gadgets

developed by Professor Agasa to help him in his adventure:


Bulletproof Glasses (with criminal tracking capabilities and telescopic vision)

Voice Changing Bowtie (for using his adult voice or imitating someone else)

Special Wristwatch (complete with flashlight, satellite phone and *stun gun*)

Power-Enhancing Kick Shoes (when he needs more power in his child body)

Even a Turbo Engine Skateboard for high-speed chases!


And don't forget, Kaitou Kid is a reoccurring rival.


Now, as much as this series is aimed towards young boys,

it really does have something for everyone.


For children?

The aforementioned gadgets, but also the Detective Boys

(or Junior Detective League, if you prefer),

a group of actual children who became friends with Conan

and, wanting in on the action, formed their own detective group.

They're comparable to the Boys Detective Club

or Baker Street Irregulars.

For teens?
The high school aspect from Conan's former life
as an adult—well, *teenage* Shinichi.
This includes his romance with Ran,
his rivalry with fellow detective Heiji Hattori
(along with *his* romance with childhood friend Kazuha Tomaya),
Ran's financially rich best friend Sonoko Suzuki,
as well as his relationships with several other teen characters.

For adults?
Well, for one,
Ran's father is a police officer turned private investigator,
and her mom is a defense attorney.
Both are currently separated (with Ran living with her father)
and are working through their relationship in the meantime.

Also, considering a good many of these crimes are murders,
it's no surprise that the police make regular appearances.
And they've sort of become an aspect of their own.
(In the Tokyo Metropolitan District, you have your usual inspector,
as well as several detectives and officers of different ranks,
who carry on their own life events in the background,

almost like a police drama.

Several neighboring districts are also explored to lesser degrees.)


Did I mention this series features several intelligence agencies

on the tail of the Black Organization?

Not just Japan, but the FBI, CIA,

and even MI6 play a role.


I guess, what I'm trying to say is, this series is very much involved.

(I like to refer to it as *the soap opera of anime*, in the most positive way.)


Now, you may look at the fact that the anime and manga

each have well over 1000 installments,

with both continuing weekly with new episodes and chapters,

but rest assured, this is a mostly episodic adventure

strung together with an overarching narrative.

(I highly suggest checking out the website *DetectiveConanWorld.com*,

a sort of Wiki that continues to organize the entire manga,

anime, specials and spinoffs into an easy-to-understand database,

even highlighting which episodes are significant enough to watch and why.)


Each individual mystery averages at 3 chapters (or 2 episodes),

and there's quite a bit of variety to them.

The vast majority of these are murder cases,

and while each one is well executed,

the quality of each case can vary

(out of over 1000 chapters/episodes,

there's only one single filler case I can think of that I flat out didn't like).


There are a few episodes here and there that shake things up,

like working to prevent a murder rather than solving one,

or even cases where the Black Organization shows up

and Conan has to act fast

to gather more information and not get hurt.


For you English speakers out there,

Viz Media has been publishing the manga since 2004,

and as of writing this, the English translation is almost at Volume 90.

As a heads up, though,

a few of the names were localized

due to Funimation's English run of the anime.


Speaking of Funimation,

they localized the first 5 seasons of the show

as well as the first 6 movies.

While a phenomenal dub (regardless of the name changes),

the studio lost the rights in 2018.

From here, TMS Entertainment and Discotek Media
worked together to localize the newer episodes and films
(with an excellent dub from Bang Zoom Entertainment)
while keeping the original Japanese character names.

As of 2020,
Crunchyroll is streaming the first 43 episodes of the series,
as well as new episodes starting with episode 754.
Select episodes have also been English dubbed
and released exclusively on the streaming service Tubi.

Of course, I believe in starting at the very beginning,
but whether you start with the anime or manga,
I believe the best entry point for anyone new to series
is *Episode One: The Great Detective Turned Small.*

This 2-hour TV Special (made to celebrate the anime's 20th anniversary)
is a complete retelling of the first episode and a half,
with new scenes and details to flesh things out.

It does a brilliant job at introducing
many of the characters we see throughout the series,
highlighting many of the cases that stand out
throughout the series' run,

and even reimaging scenes we know from the early days
with updated character personalities and animation techniques.

As for inspiration, the series has inspired
many characters in my stories, including (but far from limited to)
Ranpo Doyle from *Lab Cat*, Pat from *Eight Clouds Express*,
and the stars of *Cat Auguste Dupin* and *I'm Not a Detective!*
And yes, it did help reinforce my *more than meets the eye* mentality
(what with Conan having the body of a child and the mind of an adult).

Also, because it's still fresh in my mind,
NHK has a documentary show called *Professional: Shigoto no Ryûgi*
(known in English as just *The Professionals*),
where they follow different Japanese experts in a given field.
Very recently as of early May 2024,
they ran a special on Gosho Aoyama
to celebrate the 30th anniversary of *Detective Conan*.

I dive into it deeper in the *Enjoying Now* segment
*of SS Reed's Story Fiction: Volume 8*,
but it gave me a lot of insight
on what it means to be a professional creator,
the time, energy and passion it takes
to truly bring a story to life.

Definitely watch it, though I will warn you,

it only exists in Japanese as of writing this.

If you're a translator and you know about the episode,

please, do your part.

Use your talents to help share it with the world.

## ACE ATTORNEY

While I wouldn't necessarily call myself a gamer (especially as an adult),

I did play a lot of games (mostly Nintendo) growing up.

They introduced me to stories, characters and worlds

that have had a lasting impact on me even now.

One of my favorites,

which I discovered on the Nintendo Wii's WiiWare service

during my middle school years,

was the visual novel adventure series *Ace Attorney*.

The service offered the original three games,

and I absolutely devoured them.

Even back then, I prioritized a good story over anything else,

and each case stretched my brain in a way

that platformers and action games couldn't at the time.

Not to mention the characters.

Each and every one of them has a personality

that lets you enjoy their company

and makes you want to learn more about them.

(Which is handy for a mystery game.)


In fact, aside from the puzzles,

the characters and writing really are what make this.

They bounce off each other so naturally,

casually chatting about ladders and stepladders

or a random piece of non-evidence at the crime scene.

(It doesn't matter if they're close friends or courtroom rivals.)


The setting itself is also worth mentioning.

The Japanese version is simply Japan

and is a parody of the courtrooms of the time.


But the English version?

Set in an alternate version of America

where they had far less anti-Japanese sentiments,

allowing more Japanese to immigrate to the US

and build quite the solid foundation.

This is evidenced by the fact

that everyone is familiar with Japanese culture and mythology,

and they follow many Japanese customs in their day-to-day lives.


Remember, Phoenix's partner Maya

comes from a family of influential spirit mediums,

and she wears traditional clothing to match.

She even gives him a Japanese Magatama,

which is basically a supernatural lie detector

that he uses often during cases.


What *Arsène Lupin* was to me for literature,

what *Columbo* was to me for live action TV dramas,

what *Detective Conan* was to me for anime and manga...


...*Ace Attorney* was to me for video games.


The impact this series had on me goes beyond just my writing.

The fact that every character's name

is either a play on words or holds a deeper meaning

inspired the same naming conventions for my own characters.


In terms of worldbuilding,

it not only helped to teach me about magic realism,

but also blending Eastern and Western cultures in a balanced way.

As for real world influence, there are a few things of note.

For one, I decided to play the classic trilogy in its original Japanese.
Doing so has elevated my language skills to the point
where I can now watch J-dramas and read Japanese chapter books
without getting too much of a headache.
(Not that I can understand everything, but that's part of the fun.)

Also, *The Great Ace Attorney*
makes a lot of allusions to the Sherlock Holmes canon
(which makes sense, since you team up with the character in Victorian England),
but as I was already familiar with those stories,
they acted as no more than easter eggs.

Instead (and I won't spoil how for those who want to play the game),
the series taught me about classic Japanese author Soseki Natsume,
who (long story short) spent two miserable years in London,
and began a career in writing upon returning home.

His iconic novel, *I Am a Cat*, is referenced in the game,
and afterwards, I went to my local bookstore and picked up a copy.
(It's actually an interesting read if you like classic Japanese literature.)

Really, I think the only game that inspired me more than *Ace Attorney*

is *Ghost Trick: Phantom Detective* for the Nintendo DS.

(Which actually has an HD remaster available on all modern platforms.

Please, if you love me and you love puzzles and mystery games, pick this one up.)


If you want to play these games,

definitely start with the *Phoenix Wright: Ace Attorney Trilogy*,

which compiles the first three games in order:


*Phoenix Wright: Ace Attorney*

*Phoenix Wright: Ace Attorney–Justice for All*

and *Phoenix Wright: Ace Attorney–Trials and Tribulations*


After that, the *Apollo Justice: Ace Attorney Trilogy*,

compiling the next three games in order:


*Apollo Justice: Ace Attorney*

*Phoenix Wright: Ace Attorney–Dual Destinies*

*Phoenix Wright: Ace Attorney–Spirit of Justice*


*Miles Edgeworth: Ace Attorney–Investigations*

is one of the best games in the series,

and its sequel is basically *Ace Attorney's Mother 3*,

both in quality and...er, lack of localization...

The *Great Ace Attorney* games are good
for any fans of the *Sherlock Holmes* mythos or Victorian England,
and it actually does fix a few problems
you might have with the mainline series.

And, of course, the *Professor Layton* crossover
is good for fans of both series
or if you're a fan of one but wanna try the other.

Speaking of which...

## PROFESSOR LAYTON

So...the day is February 8th, 2023.
Level-5 has announced a new entry in the Layton series:

*Professor Layton and the New World of Steam*

Literally **while I was writing this portion of the original manuscript.**

Had I not lost my voice screaming from the news
of the (then-upcoming) HD remaster of *Ghost Trick: Phantom Detective,*

I'm sure this would've done the job instead.


The *Professor Layton* series is one
that's been a huge part of my life
since my early teen years.


It played with a lot of elements and themes
that I enjoyed back then and even now:


A European, *Sherlock Holmes*-esque aesthetic.
A gentleman and a scholar protagonist.
Adventure, mystery, and wonder abound.


Oh, and let's not forget—puzzles!


At the time,
I was struggling with a certain idea with mystery fiction
that, even today, I think is rather common:


*If the mystery isn't murder, it's not interesting.*


Not that murder makes a bad mystery (of course),
but I do find it gets rather exhausting after a while.
(While I had started exploring the world of phantom thieves at this point,

I can't say for sure if I was as well versed in the genre as I am now.)

So, when I found this series, it was a breath of fresh air.

I wouldn't exactly say I was ever crazy for brain teasers,
but there was always something about them
that caught my interest growing up.

I own a Rubik's Cube and a wooden chess/checkers set.
I was always one to play the word searches, crossword puzzles
and spot the difference games on the back of cereal boxes.
Riddles, especially, are my bread and butter.
(Sudoku is the absolute bane of my existence, though.)

It's almost like the series spoke to me on a spiritual level.

I remember playing the games in chronological order.
Starting with *Professor Layton and the Curious Village.*
I enjoyed the story, characters, and the puzzles throughout.
It was, to me, a solid A+.

Then I played *Professor Layton and the Diabolical Box.*
(*Professor Layton and Pandora's Box* for my European and Australian friends.)

This was the game that sucked me in.

Almost every aspect from the previous game was refined.
The characters were more fleshed out,
the puzzles were improved,
and the story?

The best way I can describe it, especially near the end,
was that it tickled the deepest part of my inner child
in a way not many stories had at that point,
especially near the climax.

And then, *Professor Layton and the Unwound Future*.
(Or *Professor Layton and the Lost Future*, if you prefer.)

I'll keep my thoughts on this title simple.

By the time the credits rolled, I was on the verge of tears.

If you wanna check these games out,
I say play them in chronological order of release date.
The original trilogy is self-contained enough
that you can enjoy them in pretty much any order.
The prequel trilogy as well, to a slightly lesser degree,

since the story here is a bit more intertwined.

Now, if you're playing the prequel trilogy
and you just finished *Professor Layton and the Last Specter*
(or *Professor Layton and the Spectre's Call*),
I suggest watching the animated film
*Professor Layton and the Eternal Diva*
before diving into *Professor Layton and the Miracle Mask*.
The film is set between the two games
and will actually come into play in later events.
It's also just a really great film in general.

Finally,
I wanna give an honorable mention to the spinoff game,
*Layton Brothers: Mystery Room.*

While I'm not really one for mobile games,
this game is really quite enjoyable.
It follows Scotland Yard detective Alfendi Layton,
son of Hershel Layton,
and his partner, rookie investigator Lucy Baker,
as they solve more typical serious crimes that nobody else can.

...Really, though, that *New World of Steam* trailer made my throat sore.

(Can someone get me some water...?)

## LUTHER

So when I originally published this essay,
I said I hadn't gotten the chance to sit down
and actually watch this show.

Since then, I've managed to at least watch the first episode,
as well as a few clips from other episodes that exist online.

From what I've seen, it's enjoyable.
(Not quite my cup of tea, but still good.)

It is very much a serious crime drama,
and I can definitely see the Sherlock Holmes parallels
creator Neil Cross had it mind.

...Actually, it very much reminds me
of the British mystery drama *Sherlock*
(a 21$^{st}$ century reimagining of Conan Doyle's work),
which (funny enough) debuted the same year as Luther.
Maybe with a tad less humor, though.

There were often moments

where I saw Luther chasing criminals and obtaining evidence,

and I thought to myself...


*Is he allowed to do that?*

*Is that legally, or even ethically okay?*


He does regularly struggle with that fine line,

and I guess it doesn't help when your greatest ally

is also your criminal genius arch-nemesis.


The only way I can imagine indulging

is this series is in chronological order.

## KNIVES OUT


There are currently two movies, both available on Netflix,

and, like I said in the main essay, a third film is coming soon.


I think these movies are great.

Daniel Craig does a spectacular job bringing Benoit Blanc to life,

and I think Rian Johnson succeeded

in modernizing an old formula for a new audience.

I mentioned before that the films do slightly tough on politics,

and that's very much not my area.

Maybe someone more versed can touch on the topic, but not me.


I'd say my main criticism is that it feels like

it's trying a little too hard to keep your attention,

as it likes to skip around the timeline of the story

like a stone across water,

and sometimes it made me question

where we were in the timeline at all.

(Not saying I'm against nonlinear storytelling—I do it all the time.)


Otherwise, though, the films have it all.


A large cast of stars

arriving to elaborate sets

to take art in complex mysteries for the audience to solve.


The first film has the more classic setup

of a mystery writer dead in his mansion,

while the second has the slightly more modern setup

of a tech tycoon and his friends on a private island.

(Almost makes me wonder what route the first film will take.)

Personally, I like the first film more,

though that might just be the fact

that I'm also a writer and storyteller.


The films are standalone,

so watch whichever one first tickles your fancy.


## LUPIN


So, I handled this show the same way I did *Luther*,

by watching the first episode in full

and then watching various clips online.


Although, I will give *Lupin* this.


With *Luther*,

I though the series was very well crafted,

just not my personal cup of tea.


With *Lupin*?

I wouldn't mind sitting down with this one

and watching more episodes.


Going into it,

I thought it would be some gritty crime drama like *Luther*,

and while it does very much have that similar edge,

this series is the tiniest bit more playful.


Again, it reminds me of how *Sherlock*

aimed to update Conan Doyle's work for a modern setting,

and while *Lupin* is directly inspired by Leblanc's work

rather than being a direct adaptation,

that same sense of class and mystery is there.


It does a pretty good job

translating the early 20$^{th}$ century antics of the book

into a 21$^{st}$ century story while keeping that fun spirit,

even in its more serious moments.


Once again,

the only way I can see anyone enjoying *Lupin*

is in chronological order.

# REFERENCES AND NOTES

## WHERE I SITE MY SOURCES AND CLEAR THINGS UP

# REFERENCES AND NOTES


WHERE I CITE MY SOURCES & CLEAR THINGS UP

## EDGAR ALLEN POE (Author)—AMERICA, 1841

1. David, Deirdre The Cambridge Companion to the Victorian Novel p. 179. Cambridge University Press, 2001.

2. Bonnoit, R: Émile Gaboriau ou la Naissance du Roman Policier, Paris: Librairie Philosophique J Vrin, 1985.

3. Whalen, Terance (2001). "Poe and the American Publishing Industry". In Kennedy, J. Gerald (ed.). A Historical Guide to Edgar Allan Poe. New York: Oxford University Press. ISBN 0-19-512150-3.

4. Silverman, Kenneth (1991). Edgar A. Poe: Mournful and Never-Ending Remembrance (Paperback ed.). New York: Harper Perennial. ISBN 978-0-06-092331-0.

5. Meyers, Jeffrey (1992). Edgar Allan Poe: His Life and Legacy (Paperback ed.). New York: Cooper Square Press. ISBN 978-0-8154-1038-6.

## ARTHUR CONAN DOYLE (Author)—BRITIAN, 1887

1. Sova, Dawn B. (2001). Edgar Allan Poe: A to Z (Paperback ed.). New York: Checkmark Books. pp. 162–163. ISBN 0-8160-4161-X.

2. Conan Doyle, Arthur (1993). Lancelyn Green, Richard (ed.). The Oxford Sherlock Holmes: The Adventures of Sherlock Holmes. Oxford: Oxford University Press. pp. xv.

3.    Lycett, Andrew (2007). The Man Who Created Sherlock Holmes: The Life and Times of Sir Arthur Conan Doyle. Free Press. pp. 53–54, 190. ISBN 978-0-7432-7523-1.

4.    Sutherland, John. "Sherlock Holmes, the world's most famous literary detective". British Library. https://www.bl.uk/romantics-and-victorians/articles/arthur-conan-doyle-the-creator-of-sherlock-holmes-the-worlds-most-famous-literary-detective

5.    "Sherlock Holmes awarded title for most portrayed literary human character in film & TV". Guinness World Records. 14 May 2012. https://www.guinnessworldrecords.com/news/2012/5/sherlock-holmes-awarded-title-for-most-portrayed-literary-human-character-in-film-tv-41743/

## E.W. HORNUNG (Author)—BRITIAN, 1898

1.    Hornung (2003) [1899], "Introduction" by Richard Lancelyn Green, p. xxxv.

2.    Richards, Jeffrey (2014) [1973]. Visions of Yesterday (Reprinted ed.). Routledge. ISBN 9781317928614.

## MAURICE LEBLANC (Author)—FRANCE, 1905

1.    Jacques Derouard, op. cit., p. 120.

2.    Drake, David (2009). "Crime Fiction at the Time of the Exhibition: the Case of Sherlock Holmes and Arsène Lupin" (PDF). Synergies Royaume-Uni et Irlande. Gerflint (2): 114. ISSN 1961-9464.

3.    The Guardian (2020),

https://www.theguardian.com/books/2020/dec/22/lawsuit-copyright-warmer-sherlock-holmes-dismissed-enola-holmes

## G.K. CHESTERTON (Author)—BRITIAN, 1910

1. Binyon, T.J. (1989), Murder Will Out: The Detective in Fiction, Oxford: Oxford University Press

2. Bridges, Horace J. (1914). "G. K. Chesterton as Theologian". In: Ethical Addresses. Philadelphia: The American Ethical Union, pp. 21–44.

3. Coren, Michael (2003), "Brown, Father", in Herbert, Rosemary (ed.), Whodunit?: A Who's Who in Crime & Mystery Writing, Oxford: Oxford University Press, p. 24, ISBN 0195157613, OCLC 252700230

4. O'Connor, John (1937). Father Brown on Chesterton (PDF). Frederick Muller Ltd.

## AGATHA CHRISTIE (Author)—BRITIAN, 1920

1. Morgan, Janet P. (1984). Agatha Christie: A Biography. London: HarperCollins. ISBN 978-0-00-216330-9.

2. "'Agatha Christie's secret tapes discovered". The Times. September 15, 2008. ISSN 0140-0460. Archived from the original on December 15, 2019. Retrieved June 13, 2019. Christie wrote 80 detective novels mostly featuring Poirot or Marple and it has been suggested that only the Bible and Shakespeare's canon have outsold an estimated 4 billion copies of her books.

3. Flood, Allison (September 1, 2015). "And Then There Were None declared

world's favourite Agatha Christie novel". The Guardian.

## EDOGAWA RANPO (Author)–JAPAN, 1925

1.   John H. Schroeder (2001). Matthew Calbraith Perry: antebellum sailor and diplomat. p. 286. ISBN 9781557508126. Retrieved March 9, 2015. The letter threatened that in the event the Japanese elected war rather than negotiation, he could use the white flag to sue for peace, since victory would naturally belong to the Americans.

2.   "The Meiji Restoration and Modernization". Asia for Educators, Columbia University. Columbia University. Retrieved 7 May 2018.

3.   This is a story I keep seeing passed around on secondary sources, though I struggle to find any primary sources as of writing this.

4.   Angles, Writing the Love of Boys, pp. 159-160.

5.   Kozakai Fuboku, "'Ni-sen dōka' o yomu", Shin seinen 4.5 (Apr 1923): 264-65, 270-71.

6.   Fukue, Nastuko, "Literary awards run spectrum", Japan Times, 14 February 2012, p. 3.

## SEISHI YOKOMIZO (Author)–JAPAN, 1946

1.   The Guardian (2020), https://www.theguardian.com/books/2020/feb/06/how-locked-room-mystery-king-seishi-yokomizo-english-agatha-christie

2.   Official Website, https://awards.kadobun.jp/yokomizo/

## MONKEY PUNCH (Manga Artist)—JAPAN, 1967

1.  Ancient Origins (2017), https://www.ancient-origins.net/history-famous-people/ninja-warrior-ishikawa-goemon-charitable-hero-or-violent-outlaw-008531

2.  Cavallaro, Dani (2006). The Anime Art of Hayao Miyazaki. McFarland. pp. 36–39.

3.  Brzeski, Patrick (24 October 2014). "John Lasseter Pays Emotional Tribute to Hayao Miyazaki at Tokyo Film Festival". The Hollywood Reporter. Archived from the original on 9 May 2017. Retrieved 10 November 2014.

## COLUMBO (TV Series)—AMERICA, 1971

1.  Listverse (2022), https://listverse.com/2022/03/07/ten-inspirations-for-famous-fictional-detectives/

2.  Forward (2021), https://forward.com/culture/479381/columbo-steven-spielberg-west-side-story-duel-universal-peter-falk/

3.  I've seen at least one source say Japan started airing the *New Columbo* episodes under the original title *Columbo* in 2018, though I'm having trouble confirming this for myself.

4.  Cheryl Grills, Ph.D., Enhancing Motivation for Change in Substance Use Disorder Treatment, Chapter 3, https://www.ncbi.nlm.nih.gov/books/NBK571068/box/ch3.b13/?report=objectonly#:~:text=The%20value%20of%20the%20Columbo,who%20can%20resolve%20the%20discrepancy.

## GOSHO AOYAMA (Manga Artist)–JAPAN, 1987

1.  Monthly Conan Newspaper 2014, March and April edition, https://www.detectiveconanworld.com/wiki/Interviews#Monthly_Conan_Newspaper_2014

2.  Magic Kaitou Treasured Editions 2011: Playback Episode Interviews, https://www.detectiveconanworld.com/wiki/Interviews#Magic_Kaitou_Treasured_Editions:_Playback_Episode_Interviews

3.  https://www.shogakukan.co.jp/books/09122081

4.  https://www.shogakukan.co.jp/books/09127764


## THE KINDAICHI CASE FILES (Manga Series)–JAPAN, 1992

1.  Pineda, Rafael Antonio (October 9, 2017). "'The File of Young Kindaichi Returns' Manga Gets New Manga With Kindaichi as Adult". Anime News Network. Retrieved April 7, 2020.

2.  Hodgkins, Crystalyn (December 26, 2022). "Kodansha's Evening Magazine Ends Publication in February After 22 Years". Anime News Network. Retrieved December 26, 2022.

3.  "【特報】祝・「金田一」シリーズ累計 1 億部突破!! この快挙を記念し「金田一 1 億部突破ポスター」の PDF データを無料公開します！". Kodansha. June 11, 2019. Archived from the original on June 29, 2019. Retrieved June 27, 2019.


## GOSHO AOYAMA (Manga Artist)–JAPAN, 1994

1.  コナン声優に "同期" の沢村一樹 テレビ放送開始の 96 年に俳優

デビュー 4.14 公開、映画「名探偵コナン 黒鉄の魚影」. Chunichi Shimbun. January 18, 2023. Archived from the original on January 17, 2023. Retrieved January 20, 2023.

2. Loveridge, Lynzee (January 5, 2021). "TV Asahi Announces Top 100 Manga Voted on By 150,000 Readers". Anime News Network. Archived from the original on January 26, 2021. Retrieved January 8, 2021.

3. "Shonen Magazine, Shonen Sunday Mark 50th Anniversary". Anime News Network. March 18, 2008. Retrieved November 28, 2010.

4. "Detective Conan & The Kindaichi Case Files: The Meeting of the Two Famous Detectives" (in Japanese). Famitsu. Retrieved February 7, 2010.

## ACE ATTORNEY (Video Game Series)—JAPAN, 2001

1. "Game Series Sales". Capcom. June 2, 2024. http://www.capcom.co.jp/ir/english/finance/salesdata.html

2. Ash (2016-06-24). Takumi's Class Trial. Court Records Forums. Retrieved 2021-02-10. English translation of a tweet from Takumi's Twitter regarding the incident that inspired Phoenix Wright's class trial. https://forums.court-records.net/viewtopic.php?f=31&t=32020

3. "Ace Attorney: Justice for All – 2002 Developer Interview". Shmuplations. http://shmuplations.com/justiceforall/

4. Polygon (2021), https://www.polygon.com/videos/22770046/ace-attorney-70s-tv-show-inspiration

5. Nintendo Everything (2019), https://nintendoeverything.com/ace-attorney-creator-on-initial-prototype-and-nearly-suspending-development-

maya-and-mias-origins-more/

## PROFESSOR LAYTON (Video Game Series)—JAPAN, 2007

1. https://www.nintendo.com/store/products/professor-layton-and-the-new-world-of-steam-switch/

2. Fahey, Rob (2010-10-21). "Inafune surprised Layton/Wright happened". Eurogamer. http://www.eurogamer.net/articles/2010-10-21-inafune-surprised-layton-wright-happened

3. Eisenbeis, Richard. "If it Weren't for This Book, Professor Layton Wouldn't Exist". Kotaku. kotaku.com. https://kotaku.com/5988532/if-it-werent-for-this-book-professor-layton-wouldnt-exist

## LUTHER (TV Series)—BRITIAN, 2010

1. Cross, Neil (30 April 2010). "Introducing Luther – with love to Detective Columbo". BBC. https://www.bbc.co.uk/blogs/tv/2010/04/introducing-luther-with-love-t.shtml

## KNIVES OUT (Film Series)—AMERICA, 2019

1. Jarvey, Natalie (November 18, 2019). "Making of 'Knives Out': How Rian Johnson Assembled a Star-Studded "Jigsaw Puzzle"". The Hollywood Reporter. Archived from the original on November 19, 2019. Retrieved November 22, 2019.

2. Boucher, Geoff (December 24, 2019). "Knives Out: Read Rian Johnson's Script For His Awards-Season Whodunit". Deadline Hollywood. Archived

from the original on December 26, 2019. Retrieved December 27, 2019.

3.    Canfield, David (November 26, 2019). "How Rian Johnson wrote Knives Out, the best cinematic whodunit in years". Entertainment Weekly. Archived from the original on July 24, 2023. Retrieved July 24, 2023.

4.    Topel, Fred (November 2, 2019). "Rian Johnson Says He's Still In Talks For More 'Star Wars', And That Angry 'Last Jedi' Tweets Helped Inspire 'Knives Out'". Deadline Hollywood. Archived from the original on November 2, 2019. Retrieved November 2, 2019.

5.    Chow, Andrew. "Inside the Creation of Knives Out, One of the Most Unexpectedly Subversive Films of the Year". Time. Archived from the original on December 1, 2019. Retrieved February 25, 2020.

6.    "Knives Out". Box Office Mojo. IMDb. Archived from the original on May 16, 2020. Retrieved September 30, 2021.

7.    Roxborough, Scott (September 7, 2019). "'Knives Out' Director Rian Johnson on Shifting From 'Star Wars' to Agatha Christie-Style Whodunnit". The Hollywood Reporter. Archived from the original on September 9, 2019. Retrieved September 9, 2019.

8.    "Glass Onion: A Knives Out Mystery - Financial Information". The Numbers. Retrieved December 2, 2022.

9.    Shanfeld, Ethan (May 24, 2024). "'Knives Out 3' Title Revealed as 'Wake Up Dead Man'; Rian Johnson Confirms 2025 Release". Variety. Retrieved May 24, 2024.

## LUPIN (TV Series)—FRANCE, 2021

1.   Leonard, Devin (28 June 2021). "How Netflix's Lupin Pulled Off the Perfect Heist (Show)". Bloomberg News. Archived from the original on 23 March 2022. Retrieved 4 July 2021.

2.   "This is the most-watched show on Netflix right now and it's not what you think". Vogue. 31 January 2021. Archived from the original on 5 March 2021. Retrieved 1 February 2021. that's more than The Queen's Gambit and approaching Bridgerton levels of success

3.   White, Peter (October 19, 2021). "'Squid Game': Netflix Reveals A "Mind-Boggling" 142M Households Have Watched Korean Drama". Deadline Hollywood. Archived from the original on October 25, 2021. Retrieved October 19, 2021.

···Oh. You're still here?

Well, you've made it this far···


How about a free short story?

One for the road.

# MYSTERY MAGNET

## HOW AMATEUR DETECTIVES BECOME ACE DETECTIVES

# A BORROWED RELIC



How long has it been since the fuzed...?

I still think back to that day,
when G and Ciel Auguste merged into Dupin.

One mind
One body
One spirit

I'd say I'm not sure where Ciel ends and G begins,
but, really, it's more like both ceased to be
and a new being was born from their remaining ashes.

On the one hand, G wasn't kidding.
I'm a cat, now and forever.

On the other...

...I woke up in this place.

I think it's called the...Indigo Library?

Apparently, it sits beyond the meta and physical,
holding every story that has, can and ever will be told.

I was woken up by this...hamster?
He had on a dusty raincoat and tie
and looked at me with a slight squint.
Friendly, though. Curious, too.
Said his name was Hamster Sholmes.
(Giving me strong *Columbo* vibes here.)

Sholmes showed me around the library
and we spent the time chatting.
Turns out, he also considers himself a great detective.

I often spent my time reading mysteries.
Sometimes there's a mystery that went unsolved
in my world but solved in another or vice versa.
Or maybe that's one mystery with too many answers
and I have to try to find which one is the truest answer.

Some of these I'd bring to Sholmes
and it turns out he long solved it.

Or he'd bring a mystery to me
and it's one I happened to already solve.

We've...gotten pretty competitive over time.

But, I mean, it's a friendly rivalry.
He trusts me, I trust him.
That's how it works.

So, it doesn't surprise me why he came to me today.

Right now, we sit in a room with several objects.
Many the guests can check out, but some don't leave the library.
One of the latter was a seemingly ordinary magnifying glass
with an odd quirk:

Once you pick it up,
you'll suddenly find yourself wrapped up in a real-life mystery,
and you can't get rid of the glass until you successfully solve the case.
(Y'know, like an amateur detective.)

They call it the **Mystery Magnet**.

As bright as Sholmes was, even he admits he's stumped,

so he brought me along to see if I could possibly track it.


I hop up to the empty display and take a sniff.
I know I'm not a bloodhound,
but I like to think I have a pretty good sense of smell.


Catching the scent of the Mystery Magnet
then testing the air for any possible trace...


...Oh boy.


Sholmes looks at my face.
He knows just as well as I do.


*...It's...no longer in the library, is it...?*

Want brand new
stories, essays and
storytelling tips
and tricks released
each month?


# THEN CHECK OUT···

# SS Reed's STORY FICTION!

(New volumes on the first of each month.)

**5 Short Stories**

(All of the Story Fiction genre.)

**Nonfiction Avenue**

(Where I share my personal views on storytelling.)

**Ask Me Anything!**

(Because I know you'll have questions.)

**Spotlight Corner**

(Where I share what stories, characters

and creators have inspired me.)

**Enjoying Now!**

(Because I'm always consuming new stories.)

**Special News Bulletin!**

(For only the most important updates.)

**Story Challenge Time!**

(So you can crush your storytelling limits!)

# Available DIGITALLY and PHYSICALLY

# wherever books are sold!

# SS Reed's STORY FICTION:
# Volume 8

# AVAILABLE NOW!

# STORY CHALLENGE TIME!

Make your own Tree of Inspiration! Take a story genre or character archetype you like. Find the earliest possible use of your chosen topic and try to trace the history of it into the modern day. Some paths may take a left turn, but that's okay, keep following it. You can use guidelines similar to what I set, or you can make your own if you feel you can flow better!

## #StoryFiction